W9-AZO-607

CLEAN COFFEE CUP STAINS

and Other Best-Kept Secrets

Betsy Rossen Elliot

Contents

Housecleaning

Salt is one of the basic elements of life. It's probably the first "extra" to appear on our table when we're young. In chemistry class, we're amazed to find out that the odd round box of table salt has the complex name of *sodium chloride.*

But the talents of salt are not limited to the culinary arts. Thanks to salt, you don't need a different commercial cleaner to tackle each housecleaning problem. Whether salt works alone or in partnership with other household products, grime's time is limited.

DOIN' THE DISHES

- Remove tea or coffee stains from light-colored cups and mugs by rubbing stained areas with Morton Salt and a little water. Wash as usual.
- When you can't wash the dishes right away, sprinkle with Morton Salt to keep eggs from sticking and make dishes easier to clean later. 
- Sprinkle some Morton Salt into a thermos or any closed container prone to developing odors. Leave overnight, then rinse. Repeat if necessary.
- Remove silverware tarnish by gently rubbing pieces with Morton Salt and a soft cloth, then hand-washing with Dawn dishwashing liquid and warm water.

CLEANING COOKWARE

- Make a copper-bottom pan worthy of display. Spritz the bottom of the pan with undiluted Heinz Distilled White Vinegar. Let sit until you see the tarnish evaporating. Sprinkle Morton Salt on top of the vinegar and scrub the entire surface with an O-Cel-O No-Scratch Scrub Sponge. Rinse; repeat if necessary.
- To banish baked-on food in a glass casserole dish, fill it with boiling water plus 3 tablespoons Morton Salt. Let stand until the water cools, then wash as usual.
- Get rid of grease in a roasting pan. Sprinkle with Morton Salt; wipe with a damp O-Cel-O sponge. Wash as usual.

SPIFFING UP THE KITCHEN

. . . Including the Kitchen Sink

- A mixture of equal parts Heinz Distilled White Vinegar, Morton Salt, and ARM & HAMMER Baking Soda may help open up a slow-draining kitchen sink. Pour solution down drain; let sit 1 hour, then pour boiling or very hot tap water down after it.
- To clean out debris and clear odors in your garbage disposal, pour ¼ cup each of ARM & HAMMER Baking Soda, Morton Salt, and Cascade automatic dishwashing detergent into the drain. Turn on hot water and run disposal for a few seconds.
- Pour a strong solution of 1 cup Morton Salt and 2 cups hot water down the kitchen drain to eliminate odors and break up grease deposits.

Appliances

- Remove coffee stains and mineral buildup from the glass pot of an automatic drip coffeemaker by adding 1 cup crushed ice, 1 tablespoon water, and 4 teaspoons Morton Salt to the pot when it is at room temperature. Gently swirl mixture, rinse, and wash as usual.

- Stovetop spills can be cleaned up easily if sprinkled with Morton Salt first. The mildly abrasive quality of salt removes stuck-on food, but it won't mar your stove's surface.

- If a sugary confection boils over in your oven, sprinkle the sticky spill with Morton Salt while the oven is still hot. Let it sit until spilled area becomes crisp, then lift off with a spatula when oven cools.

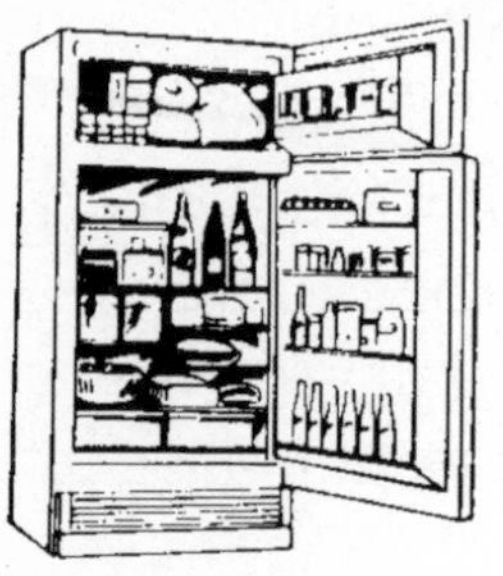

- To clean and refresh the inside of your refrigerator, sprinkle equal amounts of Morton Salt and ARM & HAMMER Baking Soda onto a damp O-Cel-O sponge and wipe down all surfaces. Then wipe again with a fresh sponge dampened with water.

- Clean burned-on food from a stovetop burner by sprinkling it with a mixture of Morton Salt and McCormick Ground Cinnamon, then wiping away immediately. The next time you turn on the burner, the mixture will give off a pleasant smell and cover up any burnt odor.

Surfaces and Stickiness

- Clean a wooden cutting board with Dawn dishwashing liquid and a little water. Follow cleaning by dipping a damp cloth in Morton Salt and wiping board until salt is gone. The salt treatment will leave the board looking, smelling, and feeling fresh.
- Wooden bread boxes tend to become sticky with fingerprints and food. You can freshen one easily by wiping its surfaces with Heinz Distilled White Vinegar on an O-Cel-O sponge or cloth.

Grease Fires and Yucky Spills

- Extinguish a small grease fire with a handful or more of Morton Salt. This method works for a burner fire or a fire inside the oven. (Use caution when putting out fires. Do not hesitate to use a fire extinguisher or call for help if a fire intensifies.)
- Cleaning up the mess from a dropped egg can be tricky. Make it easier by sprinkling the mess with Morton Salt and letting stand 15 minutes. The salt absorbs and solidifies the runny egg. Wipe away with a Scott Towel.
- If you spill a small amount of Crisco Pure Vegetable

Back to *the* Salt Mine

The Wieliczka Salt Mine, which is located just outside Krakow, Poland, has been operational since the Middle Ages. A major cultural attraction, the mine is the setting for concerts, conferences, and weddings. The mine's 9 levels of tunnels contain sculptures, murals, lakes, a restaurant, and a health clinic. In 1978, UNESCO named the mine a World Heritage site.

Like Salt Through the Hourglass

750 B.C. (approximate): The expression "not worth his salt" originates in ancient Greece, where salt is traded for slaves.

500 B.C. (approximate): Soldiers of the Roman Empire are paid *salarium argentum* ("salt money"), from which comes our word *salary.*

1559: Italians discover that ice and salt make a freezing combination . . . and ice cream makes its debut.

1694: British Parliament doubles salt tax to help fund ongoing war with France.

1777: Lord Howe captures General George Washington's salt supply.

1812: Commercial production of salt begins in Syracuse, New York, because Americans find salt nearly impossible to obtain from other countries during the war.

1820s: The Great Salt Lake in northern Utah is first explored by white trappers.

1848: The Erie Canal is known as "the ditch that salt built." Alonzo Richmond moves to Chicago from Syracuse and starts Richmond & Company, Agents for Onondaga Salt.

1863: In key moves of the U.S. Civil War, Union forces cut off the Confederacy from its salt deposits on the Gulf Coast of Louisiana and destroy important saltworks in Florida, North Carolina, and Virginia.

1889: Joy Morton gains control of a major portion of Richmond & Company and renames it Joy Morton & Company.

1910: The expanded company is renamed the Morton Salt Company.

Oil or other cooking oil, sprinkle it with Morton Salt. Wipe up spill after about 15 minutes.

FLOOR CHORES

- Try removing grease spots from a rug with a mixture of 1 part Morton Salt and 4 parts Rite Aid isopropyl rubbing alcohol. (Protect wood floors by placing several layers of Scott Towels underneath the rug beforehand.) Rub vigorously in the same direction as the nap, then rinse with water. For a larger rug, wipe off the solution with a damp cloth and blot dry.
- Immediately blot up all moisture from a red wine spill, then sprinkle the area with Morton Salt. Let sit 15 minutes. The salt should absorb any remaining wine (turning pink as a result). Clean area with a mixture of 1 part Heinz Distilled White Vinegar and 2 parts water.
- For a gravy stain on carpet, first remove as much liquid as possible by covering the spot with Morton Salt. This will prevent the greasy stain from spreading. Then follow rug manufacturer's instructions to clean. For this and other stubborn stains, you may need an enzyme detergent or a dry-cleaning solution.

FURNITURE AND FURNISHINGS

- Prevent white wicker furniture from yellowing by scrubbing it with a stiff brush moistened with salt water. Let dry in full sunlight.

- Remove mineral deposits or stains from a flower vase by wetting surfaces with water and sprinkling with Morton Salt. Wipe with a clean cloth.
- To clean and shine copper or brass surfaces, combine equal parts Morton Salt and Gold Medal All-Purpose Flour, adding enough Heinz Distilled White Vinegar to make a paste. Rub the paste on with a soft cloth. Let sit 1 hour, then wipe off and buff with a clean, soft cloth.
- Remove stubborn tarnish from copper decorative pieces by spraying them with Heinz Distilled White Vinegar and sprinkling with Morton Salt. Scrub pieces with an O-Cel-O sponge, then rinse carefully, making sure to remove all salt traces. Repeat if necessary.
- Pewter must be cleaned gently because it is a soft metal. Mix together 1 teaspoon Morton Salt and 1 cup Heinz Distilled White Vinegar, then add enough Gold Medal All-Purpose Flour to make a smooth paste. Apply paste to pewter piece with a soft cloth. Let paste dry, then rinse with warm water. Polish with a soft cloth, removing paste residue from all grooves.
- To remove a scald or water mark from a wood table, make a paste using Crisco Pure Vegetable Oil and a pinch of Morton Salt. Apply paste to mark with a soft cloth, then buff lightly as you wipe it off.
- To clean a narrow flower vase, put 1 cup of water and 2 or 3 teaspoons of Morton Salt in the vase, then shake and swirl. Let stand 15 minutes, then rinse and wash with Dawn dishwashing liquid and water.

Beauty, Grooming & Home Remedies

Salt crystals can help you live life with vigor, wholeness, and health. Stay relaxed and beautiful without spending a fortune! Salt may even have extensive healing qualities. Throwing salt over your shoulder for good luck will not be necessary!

LOOKING GOOD, FEELING GOOD

Face Forward

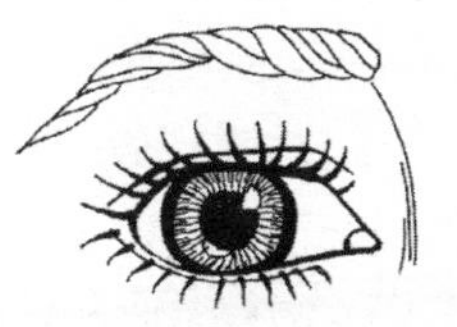
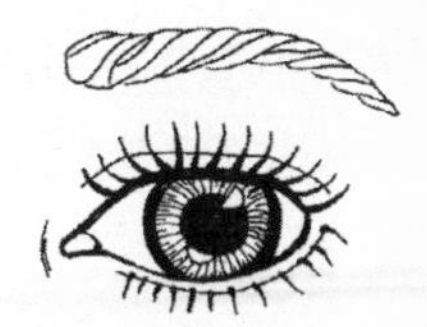

- To get rid of the puffy eyes that may accompany allergies, colds, crying, or lack of sleep, mix 1 teaspoon Morton Salt into 1 pint hot water. Dip Rite Aid cotton balls or cotton rounds into the solution, then lie down and apply cotton to eyelids. Rest quietly in this position for 15 minutes, keeping eyes closed and cotton in place. The puffiness should be gone when you sit up.
- Mix 1 teaspoon Morton Salt and 1 teaspoon Colavita Extra Virgin Olive Oil in a small bowl. Gently massage mixture into face and neck to cleanse and tone your skin. Follow by washing with your usual facial soap.
- To help combat oily skin, fill a small spray bottle with tepid water and 1 teaspoon Morton Salt. Spritz onto your face. Blot dry.

Pamper That Body

- After you take a shower or bath, and while your skin is still wet, sprinkle Morton Salt onto your hands and rub it all over your skin. Afterward, rinse thoroughly with lukewarm water. This salt massage will smooth your skin and improve your circulation. Try it first thing in the morning or after a period of physical exertion.

- Save money on gifts—or treat yourself—by making your own bath salts. In a large glass or metal mixing bowl, combine 2 cups Rite Aid Epsom salts and 1 cup Morton Sea Salt or Coarse Kosher Salt. Mix well. Add a few drops of McCormick Food Color and stir with a metal spoon (food coloring will stain plastic or wooden spoons) until well blended. Add ¼ teaspoon glycerin and, if you wish, 4 to 5 drops of an essential oil (such as vanilla, citrus, or peppermint) for fragrance. Stir again. Add more food coloring if desired. Spoon colored salts into decorative glass jars (with screw-on metal lids or cork stoppers) or clear gift bags. Add a gift tag with instructions to use ⅓ to ½ cup of the salts in a bath.

HINTS FOR HEALTH AND GROOMING

- A mixture of salt and baking soda makes an excellent toothpaste that can help whiten teeth and remove plaque. To make, first pulverize Morton Salt in a blender or food processor—or, spread some on a cutting board and use a rolling pin to crush it into a fine, sandlike texture. Then mix 1 part crushed salt with 2 parts ARM & HAMMER Baking Soda. To use, sprinkle a bit into your hand; dip a dampened toothbrush into the mixture and brush teeth. Keep powder in an airtight container in your bathroom.

- Drink plenty of water, especially in hot weather. If your doctor gives the okay, maintain your electrolyte levels (and fend off muscle cramps when exercising) by adding ½ teaspoon Morton Salt to every quart. Remember to keep your fluids up before you become thirsty, because by that time you're likely to already be dehydrated.

- Mix ½ teaspoon Morton Salt and ½ teaspoon ARM & HAMMER Baking Soda into a 4-ounce glass of water. Use this solution to gargle and freshen breath.

NOSE AND THROAT DOCTORING

- Make your own saline drops to control annoying postnasal drip. People with sleep apnea may also want to try these drops to help keep nasal passages open. Mix ¼ teaspoon Morton Salt and ¼ teaspoon ARM & HAMMER Baking Soda into 8 ounces of boiled water. Once cooled, draw liquid into an eyedropper; tilt head back and squeeze a few drops into each nostril. Hold this position for 15 seconds, then blow nose.
- To ease a sore throat and also thin mucus, gargle with undiluted Heinz Apple Cider Vinegar that has a little Morton Salt and McCormick Pure Ground Black Pepper added to it.
- The simplest remedy for minor sore throat pain is a warm saltwater gargle. Just add 1 teaspoon Morton

Salt to 8 ounces warm water and gargle several times a day. See a physician if sore throat persists longer than 3 days or is accompanied by a high fever.

- Irrigating the nostrils and sinuses with salt water is an excellent way to control persistent, annoying allergy symptoms. Dissolve ½ teaspoon Morton Salt

Salty Scripture

- The earliest written salt reference is in the Book of Job, written in about 2250 B.C. The Bible contains 32 salt references.
- Perhaps the most familiar biblical mention of salt concerns Lot's wife. When she failed to heed the angels' warning and looked back at the destruction of wicked Sodom, she was turned into a pillar of salt (Genesis 19:26).
- Salt was once a symbol of honesty and integrity; therefore, a covenant of salt was a binding agreement that was thought to last forever. For example, a passage from the Old Testament says, "The Lord God of Israel gave the kingship...to David...by a covenant of salt" (2 Chronicles 13:5 NRSV).
- In his famous Sermon on the Mount, Jesus exhorted his followers, "You are the salt of the earth; but if salt has lost its taste, how can its saltiness be restored? It is no longer good for anything, but is thrown out and trampled under foot" (Matthew 5:13 NRSV).
- Some people consider spilling salt to be unlucky. This superstition dates back to at least the early days of Rome. In the painting *The Last Supper* by Leonardo da Vinci, Judas Iscariot, who betrayed Jesus to the authorities, is shown among the other disciples with a saltcellar knocked over by his arm.

in 8 ounces of room-temperature water. Draw solution into an eyedropper; squeeze gently and breathe in the liquid through your nostrils. Repeat several times for each nostril, using 2 or 3 drops of solution each time. When through, blow nose until no discharge remains.

RELIEF AT LAST!

Mouthing the Words

- Biting your tongue or cheek can result in a large amount of blood, but it is rarely serious. To ease the pain, rinse your mouth with 1 teaspoon Morton Salt in 1 cup warm water.
- When gums are sore, use a rinse of 1 teaspoon Morton Salt in 4 ounces warm water. Swish the solution around in your mouth. If you have an abscess, the salt will draw out some of the infection. Note: See a dentist as soon as possible if you experience pain in your gums.
- As a temporary remedy for a toothache before you can get to the dentist, rinse your mouth with a mixture of 4 ounces warm water, 2 tablespoons Heinz Distilled White Vinegar, and 1 tablespoon Morton Salt.
- Rinsing with a solution of 2 to 3 teaspoons Morton Salt in 1 cup of warm water will also help relieve tooth pain.

Bites, Stings & Itches

- Work a mixture of Morton Salt and water into a paste that will stick to a bee sting or bug bite. Apply paste to affected area; let sit until dry, then gently rinse off the paste. This should relieve any itch or pain.

- Treat a mosquito bite by soaking it in salt water, then applying an ointment made of Morton Salt and lard.
- Help a poison ivy rash clear up more quickly by soaking irritated skin in very warm salt water.
- Soaking in a tub of salt water can relieve itchy skin. Just add 1 cup Morton Salt or Sea Salt to your bathwater.

Oh, My Achin' Feet!

- Relieve aching and tired feet by soaking them in a tub of warm salt water. Just add a handful of Morton Salt to a gallon of water in a plastic dishpan; soak feet for a half hour or more.
- Enjoy a mini "bubble massage": Pour 1½ gallons warm water into a large plastic basin and mix in ¼ cup Morton Salt and ¼ cup ARM & HAMMER Baking Soda. Soak feet for 15 minutes.
- If your feet are prone to fungal infections, soak them occasionally in a tub of warm salt water. Add 2 teaspoons Morton Salt to 1 gallon water and soak for 5 to 10 minutes. This treatment will also soften callused areas and help control foot odor.

Housekeeping: Cooking and Laundry

The kitchen certainly seems the obvious place to find salt. The uses for this basic product, however, go way beyond sprinkling it over your dinner plate or adding 1 teaspoon when following a recipe. Whether it's freshening up seafood or transforming vegetables, salt has some surprises for you.

What's more, salt lends a helping hand when it's time to wash a load of clothes or get down to the dreaded task of ironing. It's a super stain remover and laundry room helper!

CHEF'S SECRETS

- Adding salt to the water for cooking pasta is a good idea, but wait until the water boils. Then add 2 tablespoons Morton Salt for each pound of pasta. If you salt the water before it boils, it will take longer to boil.

- You can freeze eggs to preserve them, but you have to take them out of their shells first. Save yolks and whites, or just whites, by adding ⅛ teaspoon Morton Salt to every ¼ cup of egg. Make sure you label the freezer container to reflect the date; also indicate that salt has been added and adjust future recipes accordingly.

SURF AND TURF

- Freshen up fish just brought home from the market by returning it to its natural environment for a short time. Add 1 tablespoon Morton Sea Salt to 2 quarts cold water, then add a lot of ice cubes. Soak fish in this salt water for about 15 minutes, then remove and pat dry with a Scott Towel before preparing as desired.
- To get a good grip on a fish while trying to skin it for cooking, sprinkle your hands with Morton Salt.
- Salt will force juices out of meat and prevent it from browning. Wait to salt meat until midway through the cooking process, then salt it lightly, or wait until cooking is complete, and salt to taste.

VEGGING OUT

- Salt can help remove gritty dirt from fresh vegetables. To wash arugula, leeks, or spinach, trim and place in a bowl of lukewarm water. Add a tablespoon of Morton Coarse Kosher Salt, swish vegetables around, and let soak for 20 to 30 minutes. Transfer vegetables to a colander and rinse thoroughly.
- Get rid of the bitter juices in eggplant by sprinkling slices with Morton Salt. Stand slices vertically in a rack placed in a shallow pan and let sit half an hour.
- To poach asparagus, add Morton Salt to a pot of boiling water. Place spears in pot with stalks pointing in

the same direction; simmer 5 minutes. (Some culinary experts insist that asparagus stand upright in the boiling pot.)

'TIS THE SEASONING

- Sprinkle peeled garlic cloves with a little Morton Coarse Kosher Salt before chopping them. The salt will absorb the garlic's juice and then dissolve, which will help spread the garlic flavor.
- Morton Coarse Kosher Salt can be kept in a pepper mill and ground out as needed.
- If Morton Salt hardens at the bottom of the box or saltshaker, use a wooden chopstick to loosen it.

Varieties of Salt

Table: Fine-grained, usually contains iodine (but available plain as well as iodized). In this book, "Morton Salt" refers to the iodized variety. All other varieties are specified.

Kosher: Coarse texture, no additives; prepared using methods approved for kosher cooking.

Rock: Large crystals, less refined than table salt; used to deice roads and sidewalks, as well as to make ice cream.

Sea: Derived from evaporated seawater rather than mined; used in cooking, beauty treatments, and home remedies.

Seasoned and flavored: Table salt mixed with flavorings from herbs or spices.

Others: Specialty varieties for flavoring popcorn and canning and pickling; water-softening pellets for home devices; pool salt used in saltwater chlorinators; various industrial salts, used primarily in food processing.

- Since many recipes call for both salt and pepper, prepare a standby mixture using 3 parts Morton Salt and 1 part McCormick Pure Ground Black Pepper. Keep the mixture in a shaker by your stove.
- Preserve fresh herbs with salt. Just spread a thin layer of Morton Coarse Kosher Salt in an airtight container. Layer fresh herbs over salt (this works best with basil, sage, or mint). Spread another thin layer of salt over herbs; repeat layering process as needed. Cover the container and store with your spices. When you're ready to use the herbs, gently shake off salt to expose them. Some may be darkened, but their flavor will be fine.

LAUNDRY DAY

- Add ½ cup Morton Salt to the wash cycle to prevent colored fabrics from running.
- Brighten the colors of washable curtains or fiber rugs by washing them in a saltwater solution. Before putting in the fabrics, fill the washing machine tub with water; pour in 3 or 4 tablespoons Morton Salt and mix with your hand to combine. Add the fabrics and wash on the gentle cycle.

- To brighten faded rugs and carpets, briskly rub the fibers with a cloth dampened with a strong saltwater solution.
- If your iron has rough or sticky spots on it, turn it to a low setting and run it over a piece of paper covered with Morton Salt.

- Add a dash of Morton Salt to laundry starch to keep your iron from sticking to clothing. This will also help give a smooth finish to linens or fine cottons.

Salt Preservation

Before we had freezers and refrigerators, salt was an important preservative and one of only a few ways to keep food from spoiling.

STAIN, BE GONE!

Food and Beverages

- Remove a fresh grease or gravy stain on fabric by covering it with Morton Salt. Wait for salt to absorb grease, then gently brush salt away. Repeat until spot is gone. Launder as usual.
- Remove a wine spill from cotton by sprinkling stain with enough Morton Salt to soak up liquid. Soak fabric for 1 hour in cold water, then launder as usual.
- To clean grease from double-knit fabrics, add ½ teaspoon Morton Salt to a small dish of Parsons' Ammonia and dab mixture directly onto spot. Let sit, then wash as usual.

Ink and Blood

- Rub Morton Salt onto a fresh ink stain on fabric, then soak fabric overnight in milk. Launder as usual.
- Soak bloodstained cotton, linen, or other natural-fiber fabric in cold salt water for 1 hour. Wash using warm water and Tide laundry detergent. If the stain is still present, stretch fabric over a large kettle and pour

boiling water through stained area (if the fabric can withstand this). Wash again.

- A fresh bloodstain should disappear easily if it is immediately covered with Morton Salt and blotted with cold water. Keep adding clean water and blotting until stain is gone.

Mildew and Rust

- Make a thin paste of ReaLemon Lemon Juice and Morton Salt; spread paste on a mildew stain. Lay clothing item out in the sun to bleach it, then rinse and dry.

- Here's another method to get rid of mildew: A mixture of Morton Salt, Heinz Distilled White Vinegar, and water should remove mildew stains on most fabrics. Use up to full-strength vinegar if mildew is extensive.

- Make a thin paste of Heinz Distilled White Vinegar and Morton Salt, then spread on a rust stain in fabric. Lay item out in the sun to bleach it. Alternatively, apply paste, stretch fabric over a large kettle, and pour boiling

That Cute Girl with the Umbrella

The Morton Umbrella Girl first appeared in 1914 on the blue table salt packages and in a series of *Good Housekeeping* magazine ads. The concept had been developed 3 years earlier with the copy "Even in rainy weather, it flows freely." Tasked with finding a better slogan, the ad agency remembered an old proverb ("It never rains but it pours") and came up with the now-famous slogan, "When It Rains It Pours." As for Umbrella Girl, she's had a few makeovers over the years, the latest of which was in 1968.

water through stained area. In both cases, allow item to dry, then check stain. Run item through the rinse cycle in your washing machine and check stain again. Repeat treatment if any stain remains.

Special Challenges

- Those yellow stains in the armpits and around the collars of your favorite white T-shirts aren't a sign that you're sweating too much or not cleaning properly. These areas are just harder to get clean and are made up of more than just old perspiration and dirt. Plus, if you have hard water, the deodorant residue (and soap and perspiration) won't wash out properly. Here's one method for attacking these problem stains: Mix 1 quart water with 4 tablespoons Morton Salt. Sponge this mixture onto stained areas, then repeat until stains disappear. Launder as usual.

- Boil yellowed cotton or linen fabrics in a mixture of water, 1 tablespoon Morton Salt, and ¼ cup ARM & HAMMER Baking Soda. Soak for 1 hour.

KEEPING IT FRESH

- Control odors in sneakers or any shoes that are starting to smell by sprinkling the insides with a little Morton Salt. Let sit overnight, then shake out. The salt will help control moisture, which contributes to odors.

- Deodorize a canvas bag or any bag that has developed a musty smell by sprinkling the inside with Morton Salt, zipping up the bag, and letting it sit overnight. Shake salt out in the morning and allow bag to air out.

House and Home

"Home" generally means much more than just the building in which we reside. Our "house" can be an apartment, a mobile home, or a houseboat. No matter what form your "bricks and mortar" take, salt can help you with projects and upkeep—from managing the hardness of the water to controlling the critters in your garden.

Speaking of critters, house pets are irreplaceable and often a large part of what makes a house a home. Salt can also come in handy with them, be they golden retrievers or goldfish.

KEEPING THE PLACE RUNNING SMOOTHLY

- Toss an occasional handful of Morton Salt into your fireplace when you've got a fire burning to help loosen soot inside your chimney. An added benefit: The salt also produces a cheery, bright yellow flame.
- Save money by making homemade plaster. Mix 2 tablespoons Argo Corn Starch and 2 tablespoons Morton Salt, then add enough water (about 5 teaspoons) to make a thick paste. Use paste to fill a small nail hole, chip, or other hole in drywall or plaster. Let dry, then sand lightly and paint.

Do You Need Softer Water?

Household water can be too hard to do an effective job of cleaning. Hard water contains high concentrations of the minerals calcium and magnesium. You might have hard water if your soap and laundry detergent don't lather very well, or if your glassware or dishes are left with significant water spots after being run through the dishwasher rinse cycle. Also, your bathtub and bath fixtures may develop a filmy feel.

A household water softener works to take calcium and magnesium out of the water supply, but this wouldn't work without the addition of water softener salts, which are pellets of sodium that absorb the hardening minerals and keep the softener running efficiently.

GARAGES AND DRIVEWAYS

- If you spill oil onto your garage floor, sprinkle Morton Salt on it and wait 15 minutes. The salt will help soak up some of the liquid and make cleaning up easier.

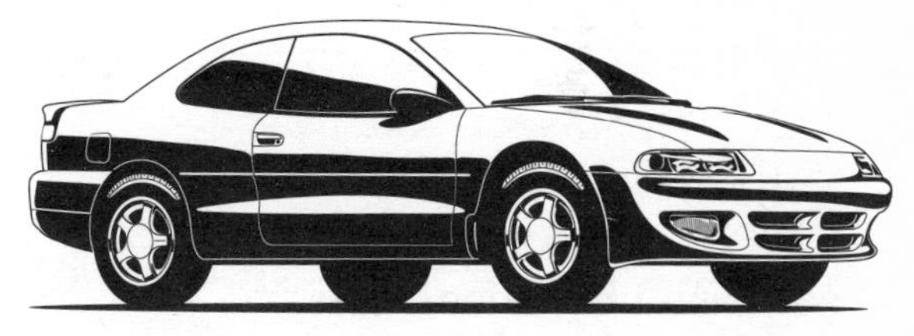

- Avoid frosted car windows on a cold morning by rubbing them in the evening with an O-Cel-O sponge dipped in a saltwater solution. Use 1 tablespoon Morton Salt to 1 cup water.

- Fill a small cloth bag or folded scrap of cloth with Morton Salt and hold securely closed. Dampen bag with water. Rub it on the outside of your windshield to keep snow and ice from adhering.

- Morton Safe-T-Salt Rock Salt is a mainstay for households in snowy climates. If spread on a driveway or sidewalk before snow or sleet falls, it will prevent ice crystals from bonding to the surface and keep it safe for walking.

- Boil 1 quart water, then add 2 tablespoons Morton Salt and 5 tablespoons Heinz Distilled White Vinegar. While the water is hot, pour the mixture directly onto weeds that creep up between cracks in sidewalks and driveways.

OUTDOOR PESTS

- A strong solution of salt and water can kill an infestation of poison ivy plants. Mix 3 pounds Morton Salt with a gallon of soapy water. Apply to leaves and stems of poison ivy plants using a garden sprayer.

- To help deter ants, sprinkle Morton Salt in areas where the insects like to congregate.

- Cabbage worms frequently attack garden vegetables, particularly cabbages, broccoli, and cauliflower. To control them, dust the leaves of these vegetables with a mixture of 1 cup Gold Medal All-Purpose Flour and ½ cup Morton Salt. Use this dusting powder in the evening or in the morning, when plants are damp with dew.

- Morton Salt sprinkled directly on a moth will kill it.

- Slugs like to feed in gardens primarily at night or on cloudy, damp days. Search out slugs at night and kill them by sprinkling them with a heavy dose of Morton Salt. Wait 5 minutes, then sprinkle them again.

Homemade Plant Food

- 1 teaspoon Clabber Girl Baking Powder
- ½ teaspoon Parsons' Ammonia
- 1 tablespoon Rite Aid Epsom salts
- 1 teaspoon Morton Salt
- 1 gallon water

Mix ingredients together and store in labeled spray bottles. Shake well before using. Spray leaves and soil of houseplants once a month.

A REST FROM RUST

- Mix Morton Salt and McCormick Cream of Tartar and moisten with enough water to make a paste. Apply to rust stains on metal outdoor furniture; let sit in the sun until dry. Wipe with a clean, damp cloth. Repeat if necessary.

- A paste of ReaLemon Lemon Juice and Morton Salt will also remove rust. Apply paste to rusted object and rub with a dry, soft cloth.

- Clean the rust from bike handlebars or tire rims by making a paste of 6 tablespoons Morton Salt and 2 tablespoons ReaLemon Lemon Juice. Apply paste to rusted areas with a dry cloth and rub. Rinse, then dry thoroughly.

THOSE WONDERFUL PETS

- The bran in this doggie treat recipe will provide your pet with much-needed fiber. In a very large mixing bowl, combine 2 tablespoons Kretschmer Wheat Germ, ¼ cup crushed All-Bran Complete Wheat Flakes, 1 cup Gold Medal Whole Wheat Flour, 2 tablespoons Quaker Yellow Corn Meal, 2 tablespoons Gold Medal All-Purpose Flour, 1 tablespoon Grandma's Original Molasses, 2 tablespoons Crisco All-Vegetable Shortening, 1 teaspoon McCormick Ground Sage, 1 Knorr Chicken or Beef Bouillon Cube dissolved in ⅓ cup warm water, and 1 teaspoon Morton Salt. Pour small batches of mixture into a food processor and blend, adding water as mixture balls up. When it becomes a ball of dough, flatten and roll it onto a breadboard. Cut shapes out of dough with a cookie cutter or knife. Lightly grease a cookie sheet, and bake treats for 30 minutes at 350°F. Allow to cool, then store in an airtight container.

- Flea-Be-Gone Dog Treats will keep for weeks, are cheaper than store-bought varieties, and make a great gift for any dog lover. Stir 3 tablespoons Crisco Pure Vegetable Oil and 1 tablespoon McCormick Garlic Powder together in a large mixing bowl. In another bowl, mix 2 cups Gold Medal All-Purpose Flour, ½ cup Kretschmer Wheat Germ, ½ cup brewer's yeast (for dogs), and 1 teaspoon

Morton Salt. Slowly add oil and garlic mixture to dry ingredients, then slowly stir in 1 cup Swanson Chicken Broth when mixture gets too dry. Mix thoroughly until you get a dough consistency. Roll dough on a floured surface to about ¼ inch thick. Use a knife to cut dough into squares, or use cookie cutters to make shapes. Place treats onto a large, greased baking sheet; bake for 20 to 25 minutes at 350°F, or until edges are brown. Allow to cool, then store in plastic bags in a location dogs can't reach. A month before flea season begins in your area, begin giving your dog one treat every day.

- If you've had a flea infestation in your home, sprinkle carpeting or rugs with Morton Salt to help kill any flea eggs. Let stand a few hours, then vacuum. Repeat weekly for 6 weeks.

- Put Morton Salt in your vacuum cleaner bag to help kill flea eggs that have been vacuumed up.

- Rub the inside glass of a fish tank with plain, non-iodized Morton Salt. Use a plastic pot scrubber to remove hard-water deposits or other buildup. Rinse well before returning fish to tank.

- Give your goldfish a little swim in salt water for a change of pace and to perk them up. Add 1 teaspoon Morton Salt to a quart of clean water and let fish swim for 15 minutes. Then return them to normal conditions.

Creative Touches and Family Fun

Salt can take a central role in your creative endeavors. Today it's a key component in an arts and crafts project. Tomorrow it will come through on those last-minute table decorations. And next week? We predict it will be stealing the show at the science fair.

DECORATIVE DETAILS

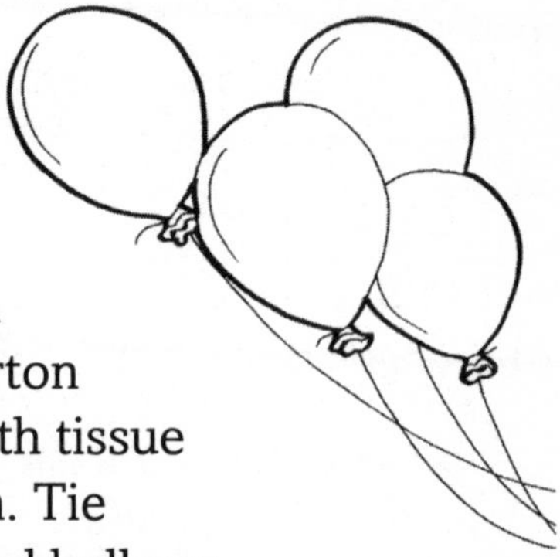

- When making a centerpiece out of helium balloons, you can create a table weight that coordinates with the theme of the party. Using a funnel, fill an uninflated balloon with Morton Salt. Wrap the filled balloon with tissue paper and secure with a ribbon. Tie helium balloons to this weighted balloon, then add any other decorations as desired.
- Use Morton Salt to hold an arrangement of artificial flowers in a vase or container. Just pour in salt, add a little cold water, and arrange flowers as desired. As salt dries out, it will solidify around stems and create a stable base.

HOLIDAYS AND EVERY DAY

- Use cookie cutters to cut salt dough (see recipe on next page) into shapes to use as ornaments. Poke a hole at the top of each shape for hanging. Place cut-out pieces on a baking sheet and bake at 250°F for 1 hour or until dough is dried out. Let ornaments cool, then decorate them using watercolors, tempera paint, or markers. You can also experiment with Elmer's Shimmer 'N Shine Brilliant Glazes or 3D Glitter Pens. When your designs are ready, cover ornaments with a transparent protective coating such as clear varnish or clear Revlon Nail Enamel. When dry, thread decorative yarn or ribbon through holes or attach wire ornament hangers.

Salt Dough

One of the most common creative uses for salt is to make a dough that is similar to modeling clay and some of the popular play clays. Salt dough is easy to make and economical! Give this recipe a try with your children on the next rainy day or during a school break.

- 1 cup Morton Salt
- 4 cups Gold Medal All-Purpose Flour
- 1½ cups warm water
- 2 tablespoons Crisco Pure Vegetable Oil (optional)

Mix salt and flour together in a medium-size bowl. Add water. If you intend to store dough for later use, add oil at this time as well. Knead dough and roll out as you would cookie dough. Add a little bit of flour if dough gets too sticky to work with.

GRAINS OF SCIENCE

- You may not be able to find fossils in your backyard, but you can make your own with this super science project. You'll need the following: ½ cup brewed Folgers coffee (cold), 1 cup used coffee grounds, 1 cup Gold Medal All-Purpose Flour, ½ cup

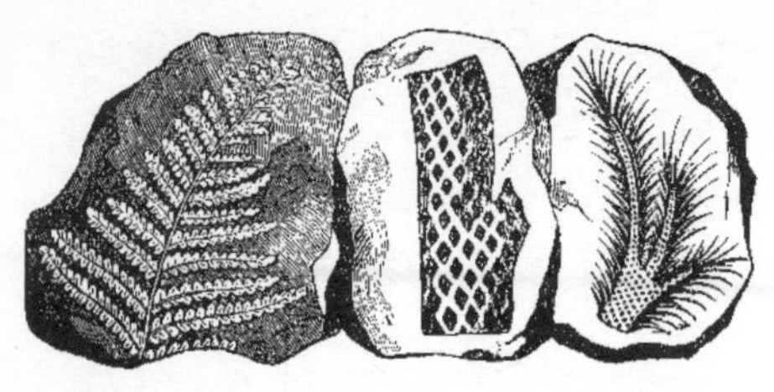

Morton Salt, Reynolds Cut-Rite Wax Paper, an empty can or butter knife, small objects (such as beads, coins, jewelry pieces, or shells), and yarn or string (optional). To make a plaster, stir cold coffee and coffee grounds together in a bowl. Add flour and salt; mix well to form a dough. Knead dough, then flatten onto a sheet of wax paper. Use the empty can to cut circles in the dough, or cut squares, rectangles, or other shapes with a butter knife. Each shape should be large enough to hold the object or objects you are going to use to make a fossil impression. Make a pattern or indentation in each piece by firmly pressing small objects into the dough. Be sure not to press too hard, or your object will poke through the back of the plaster shape. If you're going to hang your creations, poke a hole in the top of each shape—when they harden, you'll be able to thread string through the holes. Let dough dry overnight.

- Who said a garden is only made of flowers? This cool project—a crystal garden—is a sparkling alternative. It's educational too! You'll need the following: 6 tablespoons Morton Salt, 6 tablespoons liquid bluing (a laundry whitening product), 6 tablespoons water, 1 tablespoon Parsons' Ammonia, a medium-size bowl, small rocks or rock pieces, a shallow bowl, McCormick Food Color, and a tray or breadboard (optional). Mix salt, bluing, water, and ammonia in the medium-size bowl. Place rocks in the shallow bowl. Pour mixture over rocks, then drip food coloring on top of rocks.

Salt Painting

This cool art project will take your children a couple of days to complete, but the resulting artwork will be well worth the wait! Here's what you'll need:

Clear, self-adhesive vinyl
Scissors
Morton Salt
Coloring book or plain piece of paper
Watercolor paints
Paintbrush
Construction paper
Elmer's Glue-All

Cut self-adhesive vinyl into a size suitable for painting a picture (8″ × 10″ is a good size). Peel off backing; sprinkle entire sticky side with salt. Hold up vinyl and gently shake off any excess salt. Let sit for 2 days.

Place sheet of vinyl, salty side up, on top of a coloring book picture to trace an image, or place over a plain piece of paper to make an original design. Using a set of watercolors and a paintbrush, paint salty side of vinyl. Paint lightly—pressing too hard could ruin the paintbrush. Let dry, then remove coloring book page (or plain paper) from underneath the sheet of vinyl.

Glue painted salt image to a piece of construction paper to make it sturdy. Glue it either salty- or smooth-side up.

Crystals will grow in about 3 weeks. After that time, keep adding water and they'll continue to grow. Place bowl on a tray or breadboard if crystals begin to grow over edges of bowl.

Trademark Information

All-Bran® is a registered trademark of Kellogg Company.
Argo Corn Starch® is a registered trademark of the ACH Food Companies, Inc.
ARM & HAMMER® is a registered trademark of Church & Dwight Co., Inc.
Cascade® is a registered trademark of Procter & Gamble.
Clabber Girl Baking Powder® is a registered trademark of Clabber Girl Corporation.
Colavita Extra Virgin Olive Oil® is a registered trademark of Colavita S.P.A. Corporation.
Crisco® is a registered trademark of the J.M. Smucker Co.
Dawn® is a registered trademark of Procter & Gamble.
Elmer's® is a registered trademark of Borden.
Folgers® is a registered trademark of the J.M. Smucker Co.
Gold Medal® is a registered trademark of General Mills, Inc.
Grandma's Original Molasses® is a registered trademark of B&G Foods, Inc.
Heinz® is a registered trademark of H. J. Heinz Company.
Knorr® is a registered trademark of the Unilever Group of Companies.
Kretschmer Wheat Germ® is a registered trademark of the Quaker Oats Company.
McCormick® is a registered trademark of McCormick & Company, Incorporated.
Morton® is a registered trademark of Morton International, Inc.
O-Cel-O® is a registered trademark of 3M.
Parsons'® is a registered trademark of Church & Dwight Co., Inc.
Quaker® is a registered trademark of the Quaker Oats Company.
ReaLemon® is a registered trademark of Borden.
Revlon Nail Enamel® is a registered trademark of Revlon Consumer Products Corporation.
Reynolds Cut-Rite® Wax Paper is a registered trademark of Reynolds Metals.
Rite Aid® is a registered trademark of the Rite Aid Corporation.
Scott Towels® is a registered trademark of Kimberly-Clark Worldwide, Inc.
Swanson Chicken Broth® is a registered trademark of Campbell Soup Company.